T0147025

A Basket of Flaming Ashes

Acclaim

"The language; it is the language, powerfully evocative and sensuous. Ashuntantang weaves words into a beautifully strong fabric that caresses and soothes, appealing to /invoking all the senses."

Omofolabo Ajayi-Soyinka,
Associate Professor of Theatre,
University of Kansas

"This is a charming, and almost titillating first volume overflowing with romantic energy and a range of sentiments by a fiercely passionate poet. The thematic panorama is broad and the style provocatively confident."

Emmanuel Fru Doh, PhD
Poet and Author of *Wading the Tide*

Ashuntantang's poetry collection captures and shapes her landscape, sung -spoken to the unmistaken rhythm of her African sensibility. These poems are a pure delight whether read or seen/heard performed.

Pamela J. Smith, Ph.D.
Professor of English, Humanities & Women Studies
University of Nebraska

A Basket of Flaming Ashes

Poems

Joyce B. Ashuntantang

Langaa Research & Publishing CIG
Mankon, Bamenda

Publisher:
Langaa RPCIG
Langaa Research & Publishing Common Initiative Group
P.O. Box 902 Mankon
Bamenda
North West Region
Cameroon
Langaagrp@gmail.com
www.langaa-rpcig.net

Distributed outside N. America by African Books
Collective
orders@africanbookscollective.com
www.africanbookscollective.com

Distributed in N. America by Michigan State
University Press
msupress@msu.edu
www.msupress.msu.edu

ISBN: 9956-616-56-7

Front cover: Crab Orchard Lake Fall 2009 by Frank M. Chipasula
Back cover: Makanda Evening by Frank M. Chipasula

DISCLAIMER

Contents

Part II: Sundry Musings

Dedication

For my muse,

&

My sons, Ako and Tanjong

A Note on *A Basket of Flaming Ashes*

Most of the poems in this collection first appeared on my blog, *Batuo's World*. (www.joyceash.com). In preparing these poems for the print medium, I had the opportunity to re-edit some of them but for the most part the changes were very slight. However, some of the poems like "A song in the Shower" (Which originally appeared in *Batuo's World* as "Chirpy Chirpy Cheep Cheep"), and "Nfugu" were linked to the music that inspired them. These links are now lost in the print version. Also, poems like, "When I fall in Love I Talk About Buea", "Asoreh", "Bate Besong Ajaoh" and "Tambong" have been performed on video and these videos were posted on my blog. However, in spite of the absence of these videos and music links, the texture and fabric of these particular poems remain the same. In addition, "The Voice", "Betrayed", "A Buea childhood", "The Confession", and "Poetry Equals You" were included in *Songs for Tomorrow: Cameroon Poetry in English* (2010).

Truth be told, I experienced exhilarating moments of positive adrenaline rush while writing these poems; I hope while reading them you will experience the same!

Joyce Batuo Ashuntantang, Ph.D.
West Hartford, USA, 2010.

Part I: Heart Songs

A Song in the Shower

You didn't know I was listening
As you sang in the shower.
It was a simple old song
But it jolted the strings of my past.
The arrows of water poked my heart when you asked:
"Where's your Momma gone?"*
I answered in our living room in Buea
Where Mama dusted her LP brought from London.
You lathered soap and intoned
"Where's your Poppa gone"
I felt a sting in both eyes.
And answered by Papa's Grundig gramophone
Another memory of two lives I carry.
You did not see me wipe the tears nor hear me whisper:
"Far, far away"
"Far, far away"
You did not see me bury my head in both hands and rock
my body.
You came out in your towel smiling
I smiled back, got up and we chorused:
"ooh wee chirpy chirpy cheep cheep
chirpy chirpy cheep cheep chirp"
Singing my past into my present.

---

* From "Chirpy Chirpy Cheep Cheep", a 1971 song by British Pop band, *Middle of the Road.*

Yes

Petals open, nectar sweet
Eyes dimmed for sunrise within
'Tis no season for "touch me nots"
Just one word: "Yes"

I love it when I be chilling with you like this

I like it when I be chilling with you like this
You be looking at me; I be looking at you
We be playing silly
And all dem logic leave your brain and go to your legs
And your legs got no control.
Then I touch you all over the hilly and valley places
And you shake like a freedom train going north
Then my fingers be really wet
And I look at your face
And you be smiling like Jesus is your own born son
Then you give me the invite
And I take the plunge
After, I be tired and want to sleep, so you say "what's
wrong with y'all?
Can't you'll visit Jerusalem and stay awake
And I tell you,
"Girl, dem miracles and wonders inside knock us out each time
No way can mortal man ever git used to that"
Then I rest me some and go visiting again!
And now you be tired like Mary don give birth to Jesus
And I be looking at you mum like you aint got speech.
Then you ask me "what you thinking about?"
When you ask, I know logic don leave your legs back to
your brain
Can't tell you the truth 'cause my mind done already leave
the room.
So I say "Baby, just love it when I be chilling with you like this".

Joyce B. Ashuntantang

Sleep deprived

Once more you come between me and sleep
Placing a wedge in my sheets

You climb my mountains
You rest in my valley

Sleep runs to you
And I am soaked in July rain

The Image:

Why do I imagine you like this?
Under the rain, your feet muddy and dress drenched
A dim light licks my window
Your faint knock rubs my ear

But it's dry season
You are here with me- too dry
These large books are between us

When you leave, I'll close the door
My eyes hugging that image:
You under the rain at my door.

Digital Camera

Here, locked in my office
I live that photograph:

Your head cocked on one side,
And the sweet agony of your eyes undressed

The flash, like a meteor, lights your face,
Framed proof of your helpless bliss

Only Mike Angelo's brush
could strike this winning pose

But the Sistine Chapel is not here
And your 'delete' was too quick

Your Poem

I try to capture you in this poem
Leaning by the sink
Flipping pages of Meer's harvest
Pages 339 and 391 sing of Mandela's love
The phone rings.
Your towel slips
Behold the poem

The painting

Slept well?
Simple question you would say
but no words roll
to reveal the painting that is now my face

The sun and lyrics of last night
light my brown canvass.
Eyelashes stand guard over mind

Lips in gloss blush in color
as the Nordic nose
Chases scenes from my life...
Pupils ride waves of music
And ears hold court with Bona*
Left jaw cushions a waking smile

I know nothing of colors
And the sun just left
Your answer is still wet.

---

* World renowned Cameroonian Jazz musician

Nfugu*

I have listened to it 15 times already
What was there in my voice that sent you searching?
How did you see beyond my now to reach my exiled soul?

I ride the rhythm into the Atlantic.
Like slaves of old, the waves lead me;
A return trip to ancestral shores

Shoulders tell in back and forth motions
The story of the *Sosso-Bala*.**
And Akoma Mba's*** gyrating children.

I stamp the ground and my cry beckons
From the belly of balafons
My self-exile is a map I don't draw

---

*   A popular Bikutsi tune in Cameroon
**   The original Balafon reputed to be 800 years old and kept in the city of
      Niagassola in Guinea.
*** A mythic hero among the Bikutsi-dancing people of Cameroon

11

Virtual Door:

Without knowing your face
I built a home for us
so each day I wake up
Did she come? Did he come?

So now you're here
Let your words feed mine
Let your laughter find mine
Let our worlds touch

Tomorrow when I come
I'll look for footprints
Left just for me
by this virtual door

Waiting:

You said you were coming,
That was many dreams ago

Waiting has grown on me
Its fruits hang ripe and low

When you come to harvest
Pluck gently, less they drop.

Talk TO ME

I understand the language of your body
The verbs of your fingers
The nouns of your look
But talk to me tonight

Dress me up in capitals
Lowercase me in song
String your letters like beads
Adorn my waist in words

Tongue your vowels on my bosom
Tickle my brain with consonants
Cool your heat in syllables
Call my name tonight

The Award

I welcome you with outstretched arms
Your harvest is too big for the barn
The gong and drums sing your return

Children have gone to sleep
Your name on their lips.
Women have oiled their bosoms for the moon's glow
and your eye too.
Men wait to lift you off the ground

But I wait in my hut
With herbs soaked in warm water for your tired feet
*Manyanga** to massage your aching back
lemon grass to purge impurities of «road food»
AND
I saved some lamp oil to see the glint in your eyes

Tonight we will not see the moon...

Tonight!

---

* Oil from palm kernels known for its medicinal qualities

Poetry Equals You

Being with you is poetry itself.
Lines sprint in laughter, song and silence
Punctuations run riot:
Commas stretch in stride
Exclamation marks abound

Stanzas embrace orality:
Tales of folks long gone
Legends of heroes around us
Myths of bodies enlaced
Riddles of our essence

Images glide in bodily spaces
Words submerge in fall colors.
Labial sounds in legato rhythms
dance and dissolve in end-rhymes.
There's no need for scansion

Memories

Memories are clothes for naked days...
I know what to wear this Valentine's Day.

When I knew I was in love with you

When I knew I was in love with you
You were not even there.
My feet embraced the dust of your childhood
And I saw the beggar who appears in your adult dreams.
I even caressed the grave of she who gave birth to you.
In the growing pillars of what you now call home,
Your name parted my lips
And I followed my voice to the penthouse
That's where I told the wind
"This must be love; I must be in love.
 Oh snap! I am in love..."

When I Fall in Love I talk about Buea

When I fall in love, I talk about Buea
One way street into my heart: from mile 17 to Buea Town

Luscious tomatoes, color of my lipstick smudged on his shirt
Remnants of kisses falling on fertile volcanic soil

Liengu's husband, *Epasa Moto**, part man, part stone,
Sole witness to nature's surrender.

Buea rain plays see-saw;
And nipples answer the chorus on rooftops

Foggy streets clothe my innocence
Ripe bananas assuage my hunger

The taste of nyenge-nyenge** like his fragrance
lingers, waiting,

Sweat from Sarola's*** chase trickles between my thighs
While fruits hang on trees in sight

The feel of plantation rubber balls
bounces off puerile flesh.

I get lost in corridors of memory
July is no month to remember.

---

*   The god of mount Cameroon, husband to *Liengu la Mwanja*, mermaid of the Sea
** Strawberries, quite common in Buea in the 70's
*** Frenchman, 3rd Principal of Lycée Bilingue, Buea, whose compound had
    different fruit trees that attracted school children.

19

The Voice

I took your voice like a handbag to work yesterday
The sound of your "S" strapped across my left shoulder
Unleashed sensual swings in a cool breezy morning
Echoes of your baritone tickled my underarm
Flushing your "B's" through my taut body
On my desk, your tonal cadences vibrated
My pen fumbled and I wrote your name on my company invoice
I put it down and your whispers dusted the soles of my feet
Twitching and twisting, my shoes came off laughing
At lunch time I dipped my hand for dollar bills
But your sweaty moans jingled like change left in safe corners
I heard the sound, felt the bump and left it there
A little change is always good for any handbag.

Windows of My Heart

That hour when the spirit comes out to play
In the playground of exile
When shadows of the mother land
rap on windows of my heart
It is then
I pluck your love from sounds of memory

Hyperbole

Your form curves right into my heart
Your lips drip honey, I'll forgo water
Your nose is straight, it smells my love
Your eyes eat sleep, I'm awake for you
Your voice is a book, I've read every page
Your smile speaks French, Je t'adore cherie.
"All Hyperbole"
Does that mean "yes"?

Because of you

Tender moments
Fragile thoughts

Passion beats on roof tops
Laughter hugs closed windows

Dreams hide under pillows
Smiles grope beneath sheets

Someone find me!

Either /Or

Either:
Words charge through tunnels
Battlefronts of humanity rage
Targets blur edges
Words crafted in patience
Honed in persistence
Bullets for warring hearts

Or:
Poems or pistols
Bread or bullets
Which?

Teach Me

Teach me to shell peanuts
using my fingers and not my teeth.
Teach me laughter from children
sucking hibiscus nectar.
Teach me to feel the sun's warmth in my backyard
Teach me to enjoy the moon's nightly glow
Teach me to see the starry sky at night…
When you hold me…teach me!

Friendship

I miss the days when you were my friend.
When your eyes saw my words
Long before they were born
Those days when my laughter
Was a belt around your waist
Those days when the hands of the clock
Held my phone to my ear
Those days when I thumped your pages for the sun
But we pushed our friendship to the ground
Now dust has come between us.

Love after September 11th 2001

It was our usual restaurant in New York
With the usual flies

The first fly buzzed overhead
My girlfriend adjusted her *hijab**
I doubted her move

The second fly buzzed around my head
I adjusted my fear and waited
Her eyes exploded in tears

That night she sent me an email
"True love can never fear a fly"

That night I sent a reply
"Death is a fly away
I am now afraid of flies

---

*   *The headscarf worn by Muslim women, sometimes including a veil that covers the face*
except for the eyes.

27

Two Sides

Bruised spots bear the brunt of hoes
Peeling skin off dry earth
Blood oozes moistens the soil
For planting days ahead

You question, you wonder, you offer
Persistence digs fresh earth
Building mounds and furrows
Pain has become a constant

My two faced Janus
Your constant care soothes and calms
Your persistence is a blanket
Your words an umbrella

Like a baobab you tower over the past
Bruised spots repair
People grow in your bosom
Taking a life of their own

He Came Back

He came back with the sound of leaves
The birds twitting and squirrels playing

He came back with words in his teeth
The sun burning letters to the ground

He came back with insects inching the walls
The beaches calling at break of day

He came back with my heart in his hand
He came back; just like that!

Asoreh* Love

It was my way of telling you "I love you"
The white sprawling designs
captured the intricate passions of my heart.
Each time I poured *tachot*** in it
The aroma mingled with that of our lovemaking

When you dipped your hand in that chalice of gourds
My heart glowed with the smile breaking on your face.
Today, *nkwane*, your asoreh is gone from me
I saw it break in front of my eyes
Then, I knew you were not coming back.

I looked around but couldn't see
Tears clouded the pupils that dilated for you
But I wanted to keep it
I wanted the asoreh to stay
Stay in my room, in that corner
Right above my *'embo****
so when I turn at night
you'll be there, right there
You, my Asoreh love,

But they broke it
so I can be ready for another
Will I be ready? When will that be?
I am broken, like our asoreh
But our love remains, Our Asoreh love.

---

* A specially crafted and decorated dish shaped like a chalice and made out of a gourd. Traditionally meant for the father of the house, and broken upon his death.

** Soup spiced with black-pepper leaves and bush mango seeds.

*** Bed made of mud.

Monikim Dancer*

I knew I had seen you some where
But my dream was quite vague
Then I stretched on my *'embo***
And you came in full view
Those hips chasing one another
My eyes could not be still
Moonlight playing my game.

Your legs keeping the beat
Took me to your feet
I saw beads jingling in sync
Foot work artfully paced
I felt you then in my waist
As my man hit my thighs from side to side
So I tugged my *Sanja****

When I bathed in the stream
You came again in full view
The white tattoos enhanced your chiseled face
Your pointed breasts like arrows
Shot straight into my heart
I answer "yes"
My moninkim dancer

---

*   Young maidens specially selected, beautiful and voluptuous to be part of the "nkim" club. Moninkim dance is common in Manyu division, Cameroon and amongst the Ejagham of Nigeria.
**   Bed made of mud.
***   Loin cloth tied around the waist by men.

31

I wait for hunters from the hills of Apiong
I'll bring a whole deer for your mother today
And *eteuhs***** of palm oil too
Tonight you'll dance again I know
This time for me I hope.
Let me worship in your shrine
My moninkim dancer

Tomorrow, I'll tell your father
I saw a hen in his backyard
Tomorrow, I'll tell him
There's a ripe orange on his tree
And all the cowries from distant lands I'll bring
You're worth more than all I will find
Tomorrow, Let me rest in that gap between your teeth

**** Large Calabash used for storing palm oil.

Part II: Sundry Musings

Lady of the Morning

I do not remember her face but the scar on her cheek
followed me
Like colonial boundaries it made no sense
She did not see my face nor did she care
Her body like Africa had been placed on a table
Disrobed by poverty and robbed of her tongue
Her name could be Arrah, Bih or nothing.

She flung open a well of diamonds
I labored to get everything, leaving
Sweat, moans, culture, language and all

She was no woman of the night;
She was a lady of the morning.
Face washed
Scar powdered
She was ready for another
Scramble for Africa

Ngbokodems*

Dawn breaks over your silhouette
Ossing village comes in full view
Enchanting the morning of days gone by
The absence of your arm
Tells the story of your rape.
The rape of your land
The rape of your people

But your beauty is legend
Your grace a folktale
Songs still carry your name
Even our children too
Bessem, Eyere, Eneke and Efundem
Yes the names linger, refusing to die

This morning the mist cleared
Your right leg was gone too
And that pretty face has lost an ear
Then my child cried
Was it for your pain?
"Man No Rest" did not stop
So I passed you by quickly
But your image remained
Clearing with the morning light

May be when I return, you will be gone completely
But I write you down and here you will stay
And I know
You will be up again someday
When the loot is over,
The looting of our lands
Ngbokodem, our ngbokodems.

---

* Statues of "society women" made up of princesses and daughters of titled
   men who belonged to a sacred organization known as "ndem" in Manyu
   Division, Cameroon.

Betrayed
For Weka

I fell headlong for you
Your saintly face goaded me to sing
Your seminary days lured me
Your snippets of my language at dawn caught me
I matured on the wings of your new deal

But you betrayed me too soon
What happened to the ring binding us?
The "united" in our names?

I obeyed you as my lord
I draped you in colorful clothes
I made my house home
And called you "fon of fons"

Everything of mine became yours
The nectar from my tea leaves
The pods from my cocoa
The coffee from my farms

I let you swim in my sea,
And gave you my oil
You anchored at my harbor.
What else was I supposed to do?

Like your true love I stayed
Wide eyed waiting for you
No airports lead you to me
No roads can bring you home

But I sang *dimabola**
Hoping for sunrise at dusk

Now decisions excite me
And my future bugs me
Can you meet me at the M. bridge?**

---

*   *popular church song in Cameroon adapted for use usually in pro-government political rallies.*

** *Moungo Bridge which serves as a boundary between English and French speaking. Cameroon*

New Year in Cameroon

2010 flaps its wings
And flies in search of grazing land
But the fertile hills of Fako
Are overrun by plantations
Now watered by kleptocrats of Cameroes

It crawls to the forest
But saws of overseas landlords
Have betrayed the trees they claim to protect
Leaving trunks on barren soil

It swims to the blue sea
But there's no laughter here
And no mating cries
Chinese trawlers have committed murder on babies,
Even three days old.

It's a new day and a new year
like a sun-baked riverbed,
my soul longs for rain of new beginnings...

Between Airports

My goodbyes are broken pieces of me flung back
My welcome, a quilt of my fragmented self
In between are bundles of memories
Wrapped in papers
Sealed in bags
Labeled in doubt
Packed in fear
Limit: 50 pounds per suitcase

Morgantown Failed*

BB, I had planned the celebration
I had called all friends
BB, I had planned it all
The *Banquet: a Historical Drama*
Obasinjom Warrior in town
"The writer as tiger" in glory.
I was ready for the story…
Once Upon Great Lepers…
Morgantown 2007

BB, I said "At last"
ALA will see your face
I said "At last"
The name behind the cryptic words revealed.
I said "At last"
we'll flaunt you in "our" world
Basking in delayed sunshine.
Morgantown was not to be
You turned it to a Requiem
But not *A Requiem for the last Kaiser*

I still hold your other grain
The Grain of Bobe Jua
Your second poetic foray
This was '86
I read your hand
"to a fine actress" you wrote
And the ink stayed wet
drenching them in *Disgrace*

This exit remains untimely, BB
All the plans, all the hopes
We are left suddenly like *Beasts of No Nation*.
Like Change Waka and His Man Sawa Boy
You dragged Ambe and Ni Tom for the ride
To *The Most Cruel Death*…

BB, *Up above Cameroon*
You have gone but you remain our giant
In the land of the blind
Seeing *The Polyphemus Detainee and Other skulls*
So we chant and continue to gnash our teeth
Yes, Morgantown failed

---

*   The poet was to meet, the prolific Cameroon Anglophone playwright and poet, Bate Besong at the African Literature Conference (ALA) held at West Virginia University, Morgantown, from 14-18 March 2007. However BB died on his way to pick up a visa at the American Embassy in Yaoundé. This poem is a celebration of BB's life and creative works which appear in italics.

Bate Besong Ajaoh!!*

BB *Ajaoh*!! *The Ekpe* salutes
"Ooooo" the Obasinjom drools in spirit
To begin a search down here.
Your welcome on high
 in tumultuous accolades
Reverberates in ripples below.
The crowd surged and drowned my tears
The *Ekinni* came but nothing could he steal
All I had was your ink
With that we'll paint them
With that we'll build
Intricate patterns
For beautiful ones must be born
Born from your ink still dripping wet
BB Ajaoh!!! Nfor Ngbe ekati ajaoh!**

---

*   I ululate before you
** Chief of books, I ululate before you

I don't Get IT

For Maloke Efimba and Helen Mbuagbaw

I don't think I get it
One friend alive, two dead.

Her head bald as a palm
Her breast cut up and fixed

My friend is well. God be praised
Cancer, just a name. I didn't get it.

Party scene, another chats
Cancer is in, tummy chaos

Small talk, laughter, noise
Rumors, more rumors

Long call, juicy call
Hope alive, faith galore

But one morning, dark morning
News out, Friend is gone.

I don't get it. Still don't get it.

Another calls, talks, laughs
Breast dark, mass stiff

Chemo done, body weak
God speaks, Hope alive

Cancer back, no news
Death knocks, friend gone!

I don't get it. Still don't get it!

Tambong*

My hands are weary
Criss-crossing and weaving
But I weave my sleep in between.
When I lay me down on my mat,
my tambong,
my aches disappear
And when I wake
I break into song
"Tambong ayingne nor chingne kpa"
*Tambong ayingne nor chingne kpa***
And so in spirit I end my day
Once more on the mat
In sweet sleep

---

* A mat traditionally made by Manyu Women in the Southwest Province of
  Cameroon.
** Folk song in celebration of the comfort of the e"Tambong.

The Wall

Women's voices build in song
And hands stamp on the wall
Each hand a witness in color

Each hand, a support
Each hand, a shield
Each hand a pillar

The wall is a shield
The hands of women
Shielding us

Obasinjom*

The mirrors for eyes reflected the sun
and trancelike danced towards the suspect
Our long necks pushing to see
Were shoved back behind patriarchal lines

Mingling with children was our lot
But like robots we clapped
And cheered our half status

We clapped for she who had pushed beyond the line
And earned the name of "witch"
She waited for her charge
This came in guttural sounds
From the deeps of ancestral lands

Her crime "destroyer of farms"
Not as feeble woman but as elephant
She answered "yes" to all charges
To flee the hemlock platter

After all she was an elephant
Big above man and woman
Bountiful harvests in years
Reaping guilt for poor neighborly yield

She claimed her title "witch"
Then went back to her farms, only wiser.

---

* A speaking mask that has the gift of prophecy.

Witness in Nine Lines

Your eye brows
Serene and unshaved
Stand guard
Loyal and discreet
Witnesses to it all:
Stars in the eye
Laughter from pupils
Lids on tears
Closing in sleep...

Witness in Four lines

For O, More than a witness

These eye brows,
Serene and unshaved
Loyal and discreet
Witness to it all.

Personality type

Mami Njaliko was notorious in Buea
Bangles flushed her hand from wrist to elbow
She walked in strides and swayed to the jingle of her bangles
Her eyes sized the world up and down, left to right.
She wore her dirty rags as robes
And her soles like shoes
Her hair knotted from disuse
She owned her world and her wares
They said she was mad; she knew she was cool!

A Buea Childhood

For my siblings

I lick the nightly mountain fires
And taste the morning honey

The sun fights the morning fog
My clock on a school day

The mountain cries of ancestors
*"Amos Evambe, e mokala a ma ja"**

As Father Walter Stifter sprints to finish
A priest with a mountain mission.

Ewunkem curves on his legs
Tanga swings between posts

Njuma bumps his soccer head
A fatal tragedy for a star

Market days weave between the mad
Okereke and savvy aunty Sophie

In the flight of growth
Watching flying men and woman

These stories locked with secrets
Of a mountain-childhood.

---

*   *"Amos Evambe the white man has come". In reference to Father Walter Stifter, the British priest who beat Amos Evambe, the local Champion to win the 1976 annual Mount Cameroon race.*

Papa's Hands

Sitting by the bathtub
Laughing and talking with Papa
He scrubs and "beats" my school blanket
Saving my growing hands from strain
The squeezing is hard and Papa sweats
As my blanket is thick and wide
But Papa's love flows in his hands
And he squeezes with all his might
Every night at school when I sleep
Papa's love will cover me.

Go to school today, my son

Go to school today my son.
Go with the strength of an Amazon behind you
Go as your forbears went to Apiong in search of lions
My son; bring back the leopard and elephant of modern times
Go my son, the blood of kings runs in your veins
My son, a whole clan cheers and waits
Go, you child of two worlds.

Go to school today my son
 Go with the energy of history behind you
Your name is legend in distant lands
Go; decipher the riddles that shackled Kunta
Come back and liberate your kind
Go, you child of the sun,
Go, claim your realm

Go to school today my son
Go with the presence of ancestral spirits
 My son, plant your feet like roots
You belong here too, son.
Your umbilical cord was buried here
Go my son, tell your story too
 Shaka, Mandela, Etakak, tabi
Go son, claim your earth

Mile 29*

Sons, I can't answer all your Jesus questions
Can't tell you why he's white in all your books
But I'll tell you what my sons,
I have made him my Mile 29.
That stop at the bend
A place to refill
A moment to rebuild

Between J. the dreamer and Esther
I have learnt a thing or two
I try to treat men and women fair
I try to love my neighbor as myself
I covet nobody's things
 I honor my mother and father
And when it gets rough, my sons
I look up all the promises in the book,
I hide in Psalm 23
And own Psalm 100

So my sons, I may not know
When Jesus will come
It may not matter whether he's black or white
Just make him your Mile 29
Stop there ev'ry now and then
Cupped hands in unison
Drink of his wisdom
And forget the rest.

---

*   Mile 29 is a stop between the towns of Ekona and Muyuka, in the Southwest
    Province of Cameroon where there is a natural spring. Travelers who ply
    that road frequently stop here to satisfy their thirst generously.

Pictures after a high school re-union

No sisters, pictures can't tell the story
I roll them over in my hand, lifeless
Images of varied hues frozen in time
The stories of each pose remain untold

I grab this one with Anne, my childhood friend
All that is left: our laughter of one moment
The morning cake to my room is unseen
The wine from Cle, her husband, gone too

I grab the next and see my "Ngondus"
Her 12 floor room was our hub
That midnight chat over chardonnay
All lost on this paper before me

Look at this one with Flora, my love
Her face, my inspiration
Her walk, my adoration
Her feel, fleeting on this picture card

This one with my other girl, Ethel
Microphone in hand and fuchsia clad
Where's that voice that cooled the room?
I search in vain at the photo stand

See this one with Flo and Mojoko
Twin girls of my Buea past
In them I saw my sis, Emilia
my tears flowed inwards

Ah! Stories, laughter and voices trapped
I look, look, look and look
And my gaze comes alive...

USA

For my FB friends

A new work day
Another dollar day

Laps of exile
Lines of sweat

Into skin
Into minds

Grandma Christmas

My Grandma always danced at Christmas
Face aglow; steps allegro
 We called her Grandma Christmas
But she was no Christian.
One Christmas I said
"Grandma you really like Christmas"
She laughed hard and loud
Purple gums in tow
Then, pipe in-between lips
And in between puffs
She chuckled:
"No my daughter,
Every Christmas I dance
for the wisdom of women
 And the men who keep our secrets"

The Confession:

The Church bathed in silence
White walls encircled sinners

Hands clasped, knees kissing the floor
Heads fell like plants without water

It was the hour before communion
A time of forced recollection

It was her day to confess
the darkness beyond her skin

Though her sins be "as scarlet"
She will make them "white as snow"

Draped in psalm 23, she took her place
The candles flickered on her shame

I am a sinner; I fall short of God's glory
I eat flesh; I drink human blood

Oppressed murmurs sweep the pews
Hands shield faces from blight

Letters dance on the pulpit
CANNIBAL

Letters race on the dais
AFRICAN

Eyes shackled her and bodies swayed
Intoning a requiem of sounds and signs

Later she did eat flesh and drink blood
Served cold by Rt. Rev. Smith.

That Boy Obama

That boy Obama don enter the white house
But ma tears still wet the rose garden
So new days can grow

Last night Skip Gates* was arrested
He no criminal
But they put the 'cuffs on him all right.
Don't know what he be doing in them China
But child, he had no country to come back to

The other day Betty's child had no invite
15 boys on the team but no b-day card for him
Someone say he is new
That red haired boy be new too
But I guess his color ain't new

Today I turn ma TV on
 And that son of a slave owner
He call ma president a liar
He wake ma senses up
And I see Preacher King in my dream
True, the white house don turn all black
But ma tears still wet the rose garden
So new days can grow

---

*   Prof. Henry Louis Gates of Harvard University.

Prison Walls of Fruit

Dear God,
Just a few words
Before I leave your sight.

I felt ensnared
In your Garden of Eden

You gave me words
Then claimed my tongue

You gave me songs
Then kept my voice

You gave me eyes
Then took my sight

You opened your ears
But sealed my mouth

I learnt to walk
But to nowhere

You gave me man
Then kept his manhood

The one person who cared
You cursed him for good.

So I don't regret leaving
These prison walls of fruit

Yours truly,
Eve

I Cry when It's Cold

Every winter I cry
Tears bathe my face as winds slap my eyes.
At work the question is always the same
"Are you crying?"
"I cry when it's cold" I say.
They don't believe me
And now I wonder…
May be I cry
For lost totems, spaces, stories, hearths, laughs, and faces.
Or maybe I cry for me and you
Displaced, misused, abused, misjudged, dislodged!

About the Author

Dr. Joyce Ashuntantang, actress, screen writer, film producer and poet, is a major force in contemporary Anglophone Cameroonian culture. As a founding member of Cameroon Flame Players and member of Yaoundé University Theater, she starred in numerous stage and TV plays. Her full length film, Potent Secrets (2001), is an undisputable milestone in Cameroon's film industry. Her awards include, "The Spirit of Detroit Award" from the Mayor of Detroit, 1987, Cameroon Cultural Festival Awards 1989 and 1994, Outstanding Women in Action Award, Cameroon, 2002, and MOHWA "women making a difference" Award, 2010. Dr. Ashuntantang earned a BA in Modern English Studies from the University of Yaoundé, A Masters in Library and information Science from the University College of Wales, U.K., an M.A. and a Ph.D. in English from the City University of New York. She is the author of *Landscaping Postcoloniality: the Dissemination of Cameroon Anglophone Literature*, and the CEO/founder of EduART INC, a non-profit organization created to promote art as a medium for social change. She is currently a professor of English and African Literature at the University of Hartford, Connecticut, USA.

Titles by *Langaa* RPCIG

Francis B. Nyamnjoh
Stories from Abakwa
Mind Searching
The Disillusioned African
The Convert
Souls Forgotten
Married But Available
Intimate Strangers

Dibussi Tande
No Turning Back: Poems of Freedom 1990-1993
Scribbles from the Den: Essays on Politics and Collective
Memory in Cameroon

Kangsen Feka Wakai
Fragmented Melodies

Ntemfac Ofege
Namondo: Child of the Water Spirits
Hot Water for the Famous Seven

Emmanuel Fru Doh
Not Yet Damascus
The Fire Within
Africa's Political Wastelands: The Bastardization of
Cameroon
Oriki'badan
Wading the Tide
Stereotyping Africa: Surprising Answers to Surprising
Questions

Thomas Jing
Tale of an African Woman

Peter Wuteh Vakunta
Grassfields Stories from Cameroon
Green Rape: Poetry for the Environment
Majunga Tok: Poems in Pidgin English
Cry, My Beloved Africa
No Love Lost
Straddling The Mungo: A Book of Poems in English
& French

Ba'bila Mutia
Coils of Mortal Flesh

Kehbuma Langmia
Titabet and the Takumbeng
An Evil Meal of Evil
The Earth Mother

Victor Elame Musinga
The Barn
The Tragedy of Mr. No Balance

Ngessimo Mathe Mutaka
Building Capacity: Using TEFL and African Languages as
Development-oriented Literacy Tools

Milton Krieger
Cameroon's Social Democratic Front: Its History and
Prospects as an Opposition Political Party, 1990-2011

Sammy Oke Akombi
The Raped Amulet
The Woman Who Ate Python
Beware the Drives: Book of Verse
The Wages of Corruption

Susan Nkwentie Nde
Precipice
Second Engagement

Francis B. Nyamnjoh & Richard Fonteh Akum
The Cameroon GCE Crisis: A Test of Anglophone
Solidarity

Joyce Ashuntantang & Dibussi Tande
Their Champagne Party Will End! Poems in Honor of
Bate Besong

Emmanuel Achu
Disturbing the Peace

Rosemary Ekosso
The House of Falling Women

Peterkins Manyong
God the Politician

George Ngwane
The Power in the Writer: Collected Essays on Culture,
Democracy & Development in Africa

John Percival
The 1961 Cameroon Plebiscite: Choice or Betrayal

Albert Azeyeh
Réussite scolaire, faillite sociale : généalogie mentale de
la crise de l'Afrique noire francophone

Aloysius Ajab Amin & Jean-Luc Dubois
Croissance et développement au Cameroun :
d'une croissance équilibrée à un développement équitable

Carlson Anyangwe
Imperialistic Politics in Cameroun:
Resistance & the Inception of the Restoration of the
Statehood of Southern Cameroons
Betrayal of Too Trusting a People: The UN, the UK and
the Trust Territory of the Southen Cameroons

Bill F. Ndi
K'Cracy, Trees in the Storm and Other Poems
Map: Musings On Ars Poetica
Thomas Lurting: The Fighting Sailor Turn'd Peaceable /
Le marin combattant devenu paisible
Soleil et ombre

**Kathryn Toure, Therese Mungah
Shalo Tchombe & Thierry Karsenti**
ICT and Changing Mindsets in Education

Charles Alobwed'Epie
The Day God Blinked
The Bad Samaritan
The Lady with the Sting

G. D. Nyamndi
Babi Yar Symphony
Whether losing, Whether winning
Tussles: Collected Plays
Dogs in the Sun

Samuel Ebelle Kingue
Si Dieu était tout un chacun de nous ?

Ignasio Malizani Jimu
Urban Appropriation and Transformation: bicycle, taxi
and handcart operators in Mzuzu, Malawi

Justice Nyo' Wakai
Under the Broken Scale of Justice: The Law and My
Times

John Eyong Mengot
A Pact of Ages

Ignasio Malizani Jimu
Urban Appropriation and Transformation: Bicycle Taxi
and Handcart Operators

Joyce B. Ashuntantang
Landscaping and Coloniality: The Dissemination of
Cameroon Anglophone Literature
A Basket of Flaming Ashes

Jude Fokwang
Mediating Legitimacy: Chieftaincy and Democratisation in
Two African Chiefdoms

Michael A. Yanou
Dispossession and Access to Land in South Africa:
an African Perspevctive

Tikum Mbah Azonga
Cup Man and Other Stories
The Wooden Bicycle and Other Stories

John Nkemngong Nkengasong
Letters to Marions (And the Coming Generations)
The Call of Blood

Amady Aly Dieng
Les étudiants africains et la littérature négro-africaine
d'expression française

Tah Asongwed
Born to Rule: Autobiography of a life President
Child of Earth

Frida Menkan Mbunda
Shadows From The Abyss

Bongasu Tanla Kishani
A Basket of Kola Nuts
Konglanjo (Spears of Love without Ill-fortune) and
Letters to Ethiopia with some Random Poems

Fo Angwafo III S.A.N of Mankon
Royalty and Politics: The Story of My Life

Basil Diki
The Lord of Anomy
Shrouded Blessings

Churchill Ewumbue-Monono
Youth and Nation-Building in Cameroon: A Study of
National Youth Day Messages and Leadership Discourse
(1949-2009)

**Emmanuel N. Chia, Joseph C. Suh & Alexandre
Ndeffo Tene**
Perspectives on Translation and Interpretation in
Cameroon

Linus T. Asong
The Crown of Thorns
No Way to Die
A Legend of the Dead: Sequel of *The Crown of Thorns*
The Akroma File
Salvation Colony: Sequel to *No Way to Die*
Chopchair
Doctor Frederick Ngenito

Vivian Sihshu Yenika
Imitation Whiteman
Press Lake Varsity Girls: The Freshman Year

Beatrice Fri Bime
Someplace, Somewhere
Mystique: A Collection of Lake Myths

Shadrach A. Ambanasom
Son of the Native Soil
The Cameroonian Novel of English Expression:
An Introduction

**Tangie Nsoh Fonchingong and Gemandze John
Bobuin**
Cameroon: The Stakes and Challenges of Governance and
Development

Tatah Mentan
Democratizing or Reconfiguring Predatory Autocracy?
Myths and Realities in Africa Today

Roselyne M. Jua & Bate Besong
To the Budding Creative Writer: A Handbook

Albert Mukong
Prisonner without a Crime: Disciplining Dissent in
Ahidjo's Cameroon

Mbuh Tennu Mbuh
In the Shadow of my Country

Bernard Nsokika Fonlon
Genuine Intellectuals: Academic and Social
Responsibilities of Universities in Africa

Lilian Lem Atanga
Gender, Discourse and Power in the Cameroonian
Parliament

Cornelius Mbifung Lambi & Emmanuel Neba Ndenecho
Ecology and Natural Resource Development
in the Western Highlands of Cameroon: Issues in Natural
Resource Managment

Gideon F. For-mukwai
Facing Adversity with Audacity

Peter W. Vakunta & Bill F. Ndi
Nul n'a le monopole du français : deux poètes du
Cameroon anglophone

Emmanuel Matateyou
Les murmures de l'harmattan

Ekpe Inyang
The Hill Barbers

JK Bannavti
Rock of God *(Kilàn ke Nyìcy)*

Godfrey B. Tangwa (Rotcod Gobata)
I Spit on their Graves: Testimony Relevant to the
Democratization Struggle in Cameroon

Henrietta Mambo Nyamnjoh
"We Get Nothing from Fishishing", Fishing for Boat
Opportunies amongst Senegalese Fisher Migrants

Bill F. Ndi, Dieurat Clervoyant & Peter W. Vakunta
Les douleurs de la plume noire : du Cameroun
anglophone à Haïti

Laurence Juma
Kileleshwa: A Tale of Love, Betrayal and Corruption in
Kenya

Nol Alembong
Forest Echoes (Poems)

Marie-Hélène Mottin-Sylla & Joëlle Palmieri
Excision : les jeunes changent l'Afriaque par le TIC

Walter Gam Nkwi
Voicing the Voiceless: Contributions to Closing Gaps in
Cameroon History, 1958-2009

John Koyela Fokwang
A Dictionary of Popular Bali Names

Alain-Joseph Sissao
(Translated from the French by Nina Tanti)
Folktales from the Moose of Burkina Faso